SKY HIGH
NORTHERN IRELAND

AN AERIAL JOURNEY

SKYWORKS

First published in Great Britain in 2009

British Library Cataloguing-in-Publication Data
A CIP record for this title is available from the British Library

ISBN 978 1 906887 42 1

PiXZ Books
Halsgrove House, Ryelands Industrial Estate,
Bagley Road, Wellington, Somerset TA21 9PZ
Tel: 01823 653777
Fax: 01823 216796
email: sales@halsgrove.com

An imprint of Halstar Ltd, part of the Halsgrove group of companies
Information on all Halsgrove titles is available at: www.halsgrove.com

Printed and bound by Grafiche Flaminia, Italy

Introduction

Northern Ireland's six counties (Antrim, Derry, Tyrone, Fermanagh, Armagh and Down) offer some spectacular scenery. Its sea coast, particularly the Causeway Coast of North Antrim, with the world-famous Giant's Causeway at its centre, is among the most attractive in the British Isles. Elsewhere, the Mountains of Mourne, the great loughs which are such a feature of the Province, country houses like Mount Stewart in County Down, castles, monasteries and ancient sites, all combine to place Northern Ireland among the most beautifully varied parts of Western Europe.

And yet this corner of Ireland was the only part of the island to experience the full impact of the Industrial Revolution and the great city of Belfast throve as a powerhouse of manufacturing and shipbuilding. The shipyards of Harland and Wolff, for example, built a whole succession of enormous vessels, notably the *Titanic*. This prosperity was, in turn, reflected in the city's grand public buildings and monuments, which give Belfast appropriate dignity as a capital, including the imposing City Hall and the parliament building at Stormont.

Seen from above, Northern Ireland's many glories are revealed in fascinating detail – its gentle hills, dramatic cliffs, ancient towns and vibrant industry, where the mystic past mixes with the absolutely contemporary to produce a remarkably diverse and endlessly fascinating landscape.

SKYWORKS

For aerial shots with impact, look no further...

Skyworks is an independent television production company and a stock footage library specialising in top-end High Definition filming from the air. The company has become one of the world's leading HD aerial archives for High Definition video and stills.

On the television side, Skyworks produces a range of factual programmes, varying from series about history, landscape and heritage to observational documentaries and more recently drama-documentary. Skyworks has produced over 100 factual programmes for international broadcasters, including the BBC, Discovery and ITV.

The Skyworks' team is systematically travelling the globe and filming locations in the unique style for which the company has become renowned. Skyworks' archive collection is already geographically broad and thematically diverse. The company's vision is to continue filming until the world has been covered and catalogued for all to see.

www.skyworks.co.uk

The North Antrim Coast is one of the inspirational sights of Northern Ireland.

Sandy bays and craggy headlands are characteristic of the Antrim coast.

Such are the beauties of this stretch of coastline that it has been named
"The Causeway Coast" with a specific and spectacular tourist
route that runs along it from Belfast to Derry.

The Giant's Causeway curving around the top of the bay. Ireland's only World Heritage Site, it is the subject of countless legends. The most famous is that it was built by the giant Finn MacCool.

The Giant's Causeway was formed as a result of
volcanic activity about 60 million years ago.

The Causeway consists of around 37,000 basalt columns, most of them hexagonal.

A wide view of the coastline around the Giant's Causeway, stretching down to the far south west.

The ruins of Dunluce Castle, perched precariously on the cliff edge.

Dunluce Castle, dating
back to the fourteenth century,
was the seat of the MacDonnells,
chiefs of Antrim.

The kitchens of Dunluce Castle – along with some
of the servants – collapsed into the sea in 1639.

Rock arches on the Causeway Coast.

Portrush, a popular seaside resort with a pretty harbour and one of the world's top golf links.

A gas platform off the north coast – exploration continues despite the
difficulties posed by extreme weather and water depth.

Mussenden Temple near Castlerock, a memorial rotunda, built by Bishop Hervey of Derry who was also Earl of Bristol.

The heart of Derry (or Londonderry) is still surrounded by its city walls, completed in 1618 and up to 26 feet high. St Columb's Cathedral can be seen top right.

The River Foyle curves through the city of Derry. Derry's origins go back at least to the founding of a monastery here by St Columba in 546. Today it is the second city of Northern Ireland.

Agriculture plays a large role in the economy of Northern Ireland –
as well as giving it a distinctive patchwork of fields.

Enniskillen, on the River Erne, occupies a picturesque
position between Upper and Lower Lough Erne.

The monastery on Devenish Island in Lower Lough Erne was founded by St Molaise in the sixth century. Its round tower stands some 82 feet tall and was built in the twelfth century.

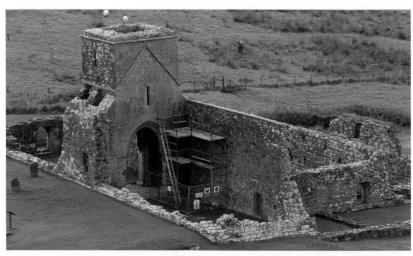

The monastery on Devenish Island was raided by the Vikings and burned in 1157, but still remained as a significant religious centre until the early 1600s.

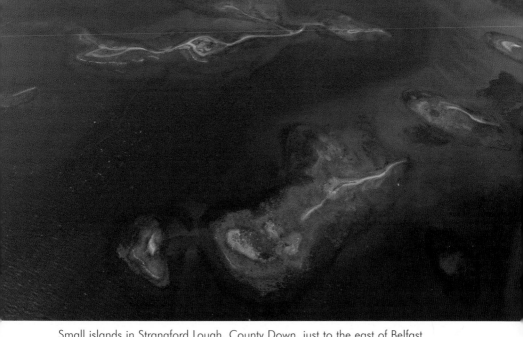

Small islands in Strangford Lough, County Down, just to the east of Belfast.

The setting of Mount Stewart House, on the shore of Strangford Lough.

The Red Hand of Ulster in the world-famous
gardens at Mount Stewart, created in the 1920s.

Mount Stewart was the home of the Stewart family, Marquesses of Londonderry.
The family completed its gift of the property to the National Trust in 1977.

The airfield at Newtonards. Although an ancient town,
Newtonards is today a dormitory suburb for Belfast.

The Mountains of Mourne rise from the southern seaward corner of County Down.

Orographic clouds form over the Mountains of Mourne.

The characteristic landscape of the south east of Northern Ireland.

Strangford Lough is a sea lough, being connected to the Irish Sea by the Narrows.

Killyleagh on Strangford Lough.

The Scrabo Tower on a hill above Newtonards, was built in 1857 as a memorial to the third Marquess of Londonderry.

45

Stormont was built between 1928 and 1932 to house the Northern Ireland Parliament. Today it is the home of the Northern Ireland Assembly.

Harland and Wolff's shipyards on the banks of the River Lagan at Belfast.
Some of the world's most famous ships were built here.

The giant cranes at Harland and Wolff are known as Samson and Goliath.

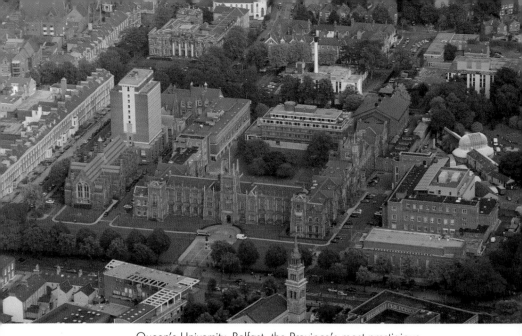

Queen's University, Belfast, the Province's most prestigious
seat of learning. The main building dates from 1849.

Belfast City Hall in Donegall Square emerges from behind tall modern buildings.

The Waterfront Hall, Belfast.

The Belfast Institute.

Approaching Carrickfergus. The town grew up around
the Norman Castle overlooking the harbour.

Carrickfergus Castle was begun in 1180 to guard the entrance to Belfast Lough.

A freighter unloads its cargo: Northern Ireland's trade is largely dependent on sea transport.

Traditional trade – a fishing boat off the County Down coast.

A panoramic view over
County Down and to the
Mountains of Mourne as they
"sweep down to the sea".

Belfast. Stormont lies at the
bottom left of the picture.

Ferries to and from Belfast. The Seacat service from Stranraer in Scotland takes barely 90 minutes; the Stena Line service only 15 minutes longer.

The Beaghmore stone circles, which were possibly a prehistoric
observatory, date from between 2000 and 1200 BC.

The landscape near Strabane.